# Table of Conter

CW00402779

# Introduction

So, you want to make money on the stock market?

Online trading has become accessible to everyone and anyone thanks to the wonders of modern technology, and the chances are you've heard the stories of people who can make a full-time living at home, all while making money through investors. Perhaps you even know people yourself who have done precisely that.

The point is that you can make a stable, full-time living through stock market investment, just like anyone can. You just need to know what you're doing and how to approach this method of financial gain. I'll say now that it's not for everyone, and you need to make sure you have your head square on your shoulders, money to invest, and the right mindset.

With a bit of practice and by taking this new approach to making a full-time income through stock market investments one day at a time, you can start making some serious money that you can actually live on. But that's just it. You need to make sure you're taking things one day at a time.

This is exactly what I'm going to be talking you through in the following chapters of this book. Each chapter is split up into one day for the next two weeks of your life where you can go from a beginner investor who knows nothing about investing in the stock market to a professional who knows everything they need to know to make money.

Right off the bat, I want to say that you may take a bit longer than two weeks to complete all the steps, or you may already be a little way in and can pick things up from the beginning, and that's okay. It doesn't matter where you are in your stock investor journey; this book is about making sure you're covering all the bases.

Every investor will embark on their own journey and will go at their own pace, so don't feel stressed out or worried if you can't get everything down in a day. This is just a program, a guideline of recommendations, and food for thought that will get you from being a beginner and transforming you into a professional.

We're going to be talking about what kind of mindset you need, what computer set up you need, how you should be looking at your finances, and how you even choose which stocks you're going to be picking in the first place. Then towards the end of the book, we're going to be looking into everything you've learned, putting it all together, and then looking forward to the future.

So, I'm ready if you're ready. Sit back, get a coffee, get your thinking cap on, and let's dive into the next two weeks and turn you from zero to hero when it comes to making money through stock market investments.

# Day One — Get Your Self Ready for Success

And they pronounced that on the first day, God created the Universe, and so should you.

Ah, Day One. The first step on your journey to becoming a stock investor. You're about to start a journey where you're going to seek full financial freedom, have an earning cap that is only defined by how much you want to work with limitless potential, and even create passive income to make money while you're sleeping. All of this is possible, and it all starts right here.

Take a moment to let all of that sink in. You are starting this journey right here, right now. As with anything significant in life, you can't just snap your fingers, and suddenly you're at where you want to be, in this case, a successful stock investment trader. Instead, you need to take small, little steps towards your destination. It may not seem like an essential step at the time, but when these little steps add up, you'll look back on your life, and you won't be able to believe how far you've come.

Let's take that first step.

When it comes to starting out on the stock market, you need to make sure you're giving yourself the highest number of opportunities to succeed. This means being prepared and understanding exactly what it is you're letting yourself into. It's this idea of clarity and understanding that we're focusing on in this first and foremost chapter.

Throughout this book, I'm going to talk about several kinds of stock investment trading in general, but for the most part, I'm going to be speaking about day trading. This is one of the more common ways of making money and perhaps the easiest to get into. Sure, like all kinds of stock market investments, there's always an element of risk involved (more on that in a minute), but there's not the same level of long-term thinking like there is with other kinds of investment. You're not buying millions of dollars' worth of stocks now to try and make even more millions in ten years. Instead, you're making small investments with small profits that add up to make a sizable income.

Here are the other types of stock trading you could want to look into.

| Day Trader | This kind of trader is a short-term styled trader that will make trades to profit from in the short-term, usually over a day or two, perhaps a week. The longest period would be around a month. |
| --- | --- |
| | These traders use technical analysis to look at stocks that will produce a profit and will sell as soon as the stock shows any sign of making a loss using the fluctuating values over the course of a day. |

| | |
|---|---|
| **Swing Trader** | This kind of trader is another short-term trader who trades over the course of weeks or months. |
| | These traders also use technical analysis of companies. They will look for entry and exit points within a stock value, but they won't use the fundamental analysis as much as a day trader will. |
| **Scalp Trader** | Easily the most short-term kind of trader, scalp traders will literally trade stocks and will only hold onto them for minutes at a time, or even seconds. |
| | If the value of a stock rises by 1% over the course of ten minutes, they buy in and sell out, and make the 1% profit. They may make dozens of trades over the course of a single day. |
| **Position Trader** | The long-term type of trader. These are traders who will invest in stocks now and will hold onto them for months, years, and even decades, buying and holding them for as long as they're turning a profit. |
| | These traders will use fundamental and technical analysis to make their decisions and identify trends to maximize their earnings. |

# An Introduction to Day Trading

As we spoke about above, day trading is a type of trading where you're making lots of little gains in quick succession (usually over the course of a day or two, perhaps even a week) and making small profits. These gains may not seem like much at the time, but when you're making five or six profits of a few hundred dollars a week, this can add up to tens of thousands of dollars of income per month.

So, let's say you invest $1,000 in Tesla stocks at 8 am. By 4 pm, the stock has gone up 5%. You sell the stocks and make $50, just like that. When you have several of these stocks on the go at once, you could be making $250 per day. That's $1,500 a week.

Now, before you get excited about making this kind of money, bear in mind that it's hard work, and it's incredibly lucky to find the same sort of growth as the Tesla stock in the example, but it does happen. The growth will vary, as will your investments, and you'll be making money in different amounts every single day.

We're going to talk more in detail about day trading investment strategies on day six but know now there are lots of different ways to invest and make money. There's not just one linear route.

Some critics will also believe that day trading is quite a controversial investment practice. Many will say that the risk is not worth the reward, but then you can speak to professional day traders who have done this kind of trading for years and have made a lot of money doing so, and they'll tell you the opposite story.

Just like everything else in life, you need to put the work in, get prepared, educate yourself, and be open to learning, and you'll be able to make it work. You just need to put the time in.

## Is Stock Trading Right for You?

Before moving forward with your journey, there is a crucial question you need to ask yourself, and you need to make sure you're answering it honestly.

Is a career on the stock market right for you?

Stock market investment at any level is no easy feat when it comes to succeeding. While there's no set right or wrong way to invest, investing requires you to be a certain kind of person, which we'll explore in this section.

Day trading, and any kind of trading, requires you to be knowledgeable in the marketplaces you're trading in. If you're not already, make sure you take some time out from reading this and getting yourself educated. The more things you know, the more opportunities you'll have to succeed.

By knowledgeable, I'm talking about having the skills to be able to read technical analyses of companies and be able to read stock market charts. These are your tools for creating an income-based masterpiece and being able to read them properly will provide you with the data that will define whether you win or lose with your traders. You need to make sure you have knowledge of the companies you're investing in or at least a passion for learning about them.

Finally, you need to make sure you have the right mindset. The mindset of a stock trader is not a mindset that everyone has. You're not born with it, but it's instead a mindset that you need to hone over time, allowing yourself to stay focused with your eyes on the prize. In fact, this consideration is so important; it's what you're going to be focusing on during day two.

If you're able to confidently agree that you have what it takes to be a stock trader, then day one has come to an end, and you're ready to move on with your stock trader journey.

# Day Two — Preparing Your Mindset

Defining the mindset of a stock trader is a difficult one. How you think and deal with any situation you come face to face with will determine whether you'll be successful or not. The successful traders in the world are not smarter nor follow better strategies than other traders. It's all about their mindset, which is why it's so important to think of it first.

So, what kind of mindset do you need? Let's explore the traits you need.

## Your View Towards the Markets

Being a trader means you need to be optimistic and positive about working within the markets you're making money from. So many traders have a bad experience and end up with a resentful mindset. You can identify these people

12

since they say things like 'the market is rigged' or 'the market is out to get you.'

Beliefs like this tend to be self-fulfilling prophecies, and if you have a negative mindset, you're going to have a negative trading experience. This is because traders will hesitate to take risks and secure their trades, which can mean the difference between success and losing their investment.

Others may sell their stocks too early with the fear of them falling out of value and not being profitable, causing them to again miss out on better, more sustainable profits. Remember this; the market is a neutral being. It doesn't want you to win or lose. It doesn't care. It has no control over that. All that dictates your success is your mindset towards it.

A profitable trader will always remember that you can win and lose traders. Even the most successful of traders will still lose on trades. It's about accepting this and moving on, minimizing your losses while maximizing your gains, which will help you make money.

## You Need to Take Risks

The very essence of being a stock trader is about having the ability to take calculated risks. If you're not cut out for taking risks, then you're not in the right mindset, but this will be reflected throughout your life. When you ask someone on a date or to marry them, or you're trying something new at your favorite restaurant, these are all forms of taking risk.

Being a stock trader is all about taking mindful risks and being able to lean into the uncertainty of a trade. Sure, there are going to be safer risks than others and trades that are more likely to be successful, but there will come the point where you need to take a bold risk, and you need to ensure you're in the right mindset to take it.

## You Need to Be Sound of Mind Financially

If you have problems managing your money, you have a mindset of 'money doesn't matter' or you love to spend lucratively, then stock trading may not be for you. The best stock traders will see and strictly treat money as a resource to make money. Money needs to be viewed as an asset for your business, even if that business is just you sat at a computer at home.

Being a stock trader does not mean you're gambling your money away. It's not like being in Vegas, and you're throwing thousands of dollars into an investment and hoping for the best. Stock traders are calculated, disciplined, and focused on their objectives and how to get there, and you need to be too.

## You Cannot be Emotional

The final point you need to think about is how much of an emotional person you are, or how dramatically you react towards certain things. If something happens in your life, that's either good or bad, how can you deal with it in a sound and stable state of mind?

Whether you're winning big or losing hard as a stock trader, you need to make sure you're remaining grounded and disciplined at all times. The mind is a beautiful thing, but it can also be your worst enemy. When you're losing hard, your first instinct may be to freak out and change your strategy because it's clearly not working, and this is where people end up ending their careers. In singular moments like that.

Instead, you need to be able to detach yourself from the situation and stick to your strategy, even when times are hard. It's statistically guaranteed that at some point during your career, you're going to have the worst losing streak you've ever had, as well as the most tremendous winning streak. You need to remain neutral through both and every time in-between.

## You Need to Be Disciplined

Trading in the stock market world is full of highs and lows, and there's no doubt about it, but you're going to experience both. Some days will be quiet with not much happening, and some days will chaotic, and that's an understatement.

While it's important not to let your emotions get in the way, it's more important to be disciplined enough to stick to your strategy, even when it seems as though the world is going crazy.

When you're winning, it can be so tempting to deviate from your strategy and think about pouring more money into a stock to maximizing your earnings. However, it's getting carried away with mistakes like this that are going to cost you in the long term. It may work once, but if you keep doing it, you're going to trip.

Likewise, if you're losing hard, it can be tempting to believe your strategy isn't working, and you need to do something drastic. This is where mistakes will happen because you're making decisions based on the emotions you're feeling. Even when the going gets tough, you need to ensure you're disciplined enough to stick with your strategy.

Practice discipline wherever you can and make sure you're working with your plan as much as you can. Trust the process, and be mindful of how you approach trading. Always remain focused and never act from an emotional standpoint.

When you're trying to make money in the stock market world, you need to make sure you can keep your head on your shoulders and your mind on the job. Before you take any steps further on your path to be a trader and earning passive income, you need to make sure your mindset is in the right place.

At the end of the day, your psychological mindset will always determine whether you're a successful trader or not.

# Day Three — Prepping Your Capital

Okay, so you've spent the last couple of days organizing your life and your mindset, and at this point you should be in a headspace where you're ready to start trading. Your mind is in the right place, or you're at least working on it, and you're ready to start rolling the ball that will kickstart your career in the stock market.

Let's make it happen.

First things first, you're going to need some money to trade with. Now, when you're starting any kind of business, you need capital. This is money you invest into your business to make money. If you're creating a product, you'll spend this money producing units, marketing, and delivering the product in the best possible way. You sell units, and you make your money back.

The trading world works similarly. You need to invest money to make money, which means you need money to start with, which is what you're going to be doing on day three.

Starting with the basics, you need to make sure you have enough capital to cover any potential losses you're going to make at the beginning of your trading career. For example, out of your first ten days of actually trading, you may lose on the first nine days (disheartening, I know), but then you actually make a profit on all the investments on the tenth day, meaning you're not at a loss. This means you need to have the capital to see you through those nine days.

If you've read Trade Your Way to Financial Freedom, by Van Tharp, you'll know he suggests that you start with around $100,000 in capital before you start, but the chances are you're not going to have this amount, especially if you're day trading.

Yes, you can start with smaller amounts, but you're not going to want to quit your day job until you start snowballing that initial capital. Let's say you start with $25,000. You spend four hours of your day trading, and over the course of a year, you turn this into $80,000. You've done really well, and now you can start transferring yourself from your job into a full-time career.

However, if you're starting with $100,000, as recommended by Tharp, then you can invest $50,000, make $100,000, and still have $25,000 to fall back on. Basically, the more capital you're starting with, the better. If you're day trading, Tharp recommends you keep around $10,000 in your trading account at all times.

## Where to Secure Your Capital

So, where exactly are you going to get this starting capital?

The most common place is through savings. You may have savings built up over the years, which you have now reached a point where you can start using them to invest. You may wish to seek your initial investment from someone, like an investor or a bank. I wouldn't recommend this approach because if you lose all the money, then you won't be able to pay it back, and this can lead you into deep financial trouble, but the opportunity is always there.

You may also want to acquire the money from a friend or family member. Where you get your initial investment is up to you, and you may get it from one or multiple places from the list above. The point you'll want to remember most importantly is that you're financially secure outside of this investment.

Investing money on the stock market is a form of business, which means it should impact your personal life. If you're selling everything to make money on the stock market, how are you going to live and pay your bills and for your computer and electricity? I'm not saying you can't, because you need to make the decision that's right for you, but when it comes to stock market money, you might not make a return for some time, so you need to ensure you're covered until the money starts coming in.

This is especially the case when you're starting out, which is why I'm going to talk you through some key things to remember when it comes to organizing your finances.

## Setting Up Your Finances First

So, you don't want to mess up your life by beginning a stock market career. The stock market takes the investment of both time and money, so you can't just trade for a bit and hope the best. The most successful traders, even those day trading who make multiple trades in a day, will only make money over the long term.

Remember how we spoke about lots of little wins over a long period of time makes up a big win.

This means you need to protect yourself from having financial problems. Ideally, you'll want to start trading a couple of hours a day, perhaps a bit before and a bit after work, and work on building up your portfolio by investing your savings. Then, once your portfolio has become self-sufficient and you can start paying yourself a decent wage, then you can quit the job you have now, and away you go. Start small and work your way up.

You can quit your job and go full-time into a stock market career, but I would only recommend this if you have experience and know what you're doing, because if it doesn't work out and stock market trading isn't for you, then you may be left in a bit of a pickle.

You'll also want to save up and get yourself an emergency fund. The top investors will always recommend this tactic to new traders, and it basically refers to making a savings account that holds money for you to use as and when you need it, but mostly in an emergency situation.

This way, while you're building up your portfolio and starting to snowball your earnings, if your car breaks down, you need to pay for a house repair or an unexpected bill, or money gets tight, you have finances to fall back on. Most people would recommend saving up around three months' worth of money of what it costs for you to live.

For example, if you spend roughly $2,000 a month on living, you'll need to save $6,000 into an emergency fund savings account. You then need to save the $10,000 you're starting with on top of that.

Once you're happy with your financial situation, you've covered all the basics, and you're ready to move forward, it's time to focus on setting up your set up.

# Day Four — Setting Up Your Set-Up

Okay, so you've got your mindset ready and in the zone. Check. You've got your finances sorted, and your investment capital is ready to go. Check. You're ready to start making money on the stock market as a trader. Check. Now all you need is the right tools for the job, which is exactly what we're going to be covering in this chapter.

No need to fuss around here. Let's jump straight into it.

## Creating Your Workstation

The absolute most crucial thing you're going to need is a computer. This is so you can access your finances and your broker account (more on brokerage accounts in a bit), and an internet connection.

Since stock trading can be a laborious and mentally exhausting (although rewarding) career, you're probably going to want your own space to set everything up. You could convert a shed in your garden or a room in your home and transform them into your office. Either way, you're going to want your own space where you're not going to be distracted.

Once you've found your space, and you're ready to start setting everything up, set up your computer first on a desk, and make sure you get a comfortable desk with a chair that's supportive for your posture. It's ideal for your health and posture to get a standing desk since you'll be sitting in front of a computer all day, and that's not the healthiest way to spend a day.

You don't need the most fantastic computer in the world, but you don't want to go for the cheapest option you can find. You'll want a midrange computer since you'll be running stock market software like chart software and the sorts, and you don't want your computer to be unable to run it in a year or so when the software inevitably updates.

For any other career, a slow computer could work fine, but when you're trading and examining stocks literally changing value by the minute, you can't afford to have a computer that's going to let you down.

The same logic applies to your internet connection.

You don't want to be halfway through a trade, and suddenly your internet cuts out. Not only is this incredibly unsafe for your finances since it can bug where your money is going and can even compromise the security of your account. Again, you can't afford to have your internet connection lag or crash at any time.

The chances are you've already got yourself a decent internet package, which is how you watch platforms like YouTube or Netflix, but just check to make sure everything is going to run. If you already experience lagging on your internet, then it's probably time to update before you start your trading career.

## Choosing Your Stockbroker Software

There are many different trading platforms out there, and which one you choose will really depend on what suits you and what you're trying to achieve. There's no right or wrong option here, so your best bet is to download a few and simply try them out.

Most software packages will allow you to explore their software for free, and they'll just take a commission from your trades, so you don't need to worry about any sign-up fees or package costs. You may need to make a minimum deposit, which you should probably avoid in case you don't want to work with the broker, so always check first to see if there's a demo version available.

You'll also want to see what features are available to suit you. The chances are you'll probably change your trading platform several times throughout your career, so just start with a basic one, master the features and what you're doing, and then upgrade when you need to.

And with that, you should have everything set up and ready to go. This is a super exciting time because you're just about ready to trade. In the following chapter, we're going to explore the final bits and pieces you need to know before we get to the juicy bit.

# Day Five — Everything Else You Need to Know Before You Trade

From what you've learned so far, you should know everything you need to know that has now left you in a position where you're ready to start trading. Everything is set up and ready to go. However, there are a few bits and pieces, more like tips and tricks, you need to know first, and that's what I'm dedicating this chapter too.

## Think About Your Security

No, I'm not talking about stock market securities, but I'm talking about the security of your broker accounts. You need to make sure you're thinking about setting strong, randomized passwords on your account that nobody can guess or break into. Think of this way; you could hold broker accounts with tens of thousands of dollars in them. Are you really going to set your password as your birthday date?

Don't let people get access to your accounts.

Likewise, if you're planning to work in a café or remote work, then you need to make sure you're using a VPN to protect your internet connection. If you're using a public Wi-Fi connection, then people can see what data you're sending from your computer, which means they can see all the money you're transferring.

Protect yourself and your investments by investing in internet security, virus protection, and a VPN to protect your internet connection, especially if you're working while you're out and about.

## Take Days Off

It can be exhilarating when you're working for yourself, and you really start making money in the stock market. It's easy to simply feel like you can invest all your time here working, and you'll just keep on making money. The more hours you put in, the more money you'll make, right?

Well, not entirely. It's essential to make sure you're taking days off, and I mean full days off, especially with a career in the stock market. If you're tired and unrested, you'll find you won't be grounded or level-headed when you're making decisions, and you're much more likely to make a bad decision that's going to cost you.

The best way to avoid this happening is simply to take some days off and only work during set hours. Of course, you can only actually trade during the trading hours specified by the stock market. Still, it's so easy to spend hour after hour until the early hours of the morning researching companies, reading the news, and watching different stocks.

Switch off your computer, eat something, drink water, take a walk, and sleep properly. You'll perform at a much higher level if you're able to do all of these things.

## Don't Put All Your Eggs in One Basket

A top tip to remember. Diversify your portfolio to increase your chances of succeeding and minimizing your losses. This applies to all strategies, so start etching this into your mind now. If you put 100% of your capital into one stock. If you win, that's great. If you lose, you've lost everything. This is not minimizing your losses.

Instead, if you put 10% of your budget into ten different stocks, then your profits will be varied, as will your losses, and you can move things around as you go, making sure you're riding the highs and reducing the lows as much as you can.

Now, we're going to talk more about strategies next, because of course, stock market investment isn't as easy as that, but that's the main idea you'll want to drill in.

As a rule of thumb, most day traders will set a daily limit to what they're allowing themselves to spend and then will only spend between 2% and 10% of their daily budget on a single trade. This is an excellent habit to start with because it will teach you self-control over your finances and will help you to build a diverse portfolio naturally.

## Reinvest Your Earnings

The proper way to make money on your money is to compound the profits you make. Unless you desperately need to withdraw money from your account to live on, it's always worth reinvesting the money you make into more stocks and then making more money off this money.

Over the long-term, this is the exact approach you'll need to take when you want to make it big and secure financial freedom for yourself. Let's say, for example, you start with $10,000 and earn $5,000 over a year. You make 50%, just as an example to keep things simple.

Next year, you reinvest that $15,000 and make another 50% in total, meaning you now have $22,500. You reinvest this and make another 50%, which means you have $33,750. This is a basic example of how compounding your profit works and why it's so crucial if you want to make big money.

## Try Different Strategies and Stick to It

The final tip I can give you before we dive headfirst into the technicalities of becoming an investor on the stock market is to research as many strategies as you can and then figure out which one is best for you. Then, once you're happy, you need to make sure you're sticking with this strategy, which means marrying this strategy. You need to stay with it through thick and thin.

There will be good times in your career, and there will be bad times. When you're winning, it can be tempting to ride the hype and go all in, but this isn't your strategy, and this is where things will quickly go wrong. Just to be clear, always stick to your strategy!

Which strategy you choose, however, is entirely up to you. I'm going to detail a few throughout this book, so use this as a starting point, but don't believe these are the only strategies. Take your time and research which you like the look before fully committing and going for it.

# Day Six — Creating Your Investment Strategy

Okay. This is the chapter you've been waiting for. It's time to start looking into strategies on how you actually make money. You've got your investment, and everything is set up and ready to go. You've deposited money into your account, and you're ready to make a trade. Right off the bat, you're not going to want to log on and just start buying stocks here, there, and everywhere. That's how you lose.

Instead, you need a strategy to work to, and I've spoken so much about this already, so I'm sure you won't need any introduction. There are many strategies out there, and you can pick any you like the look of, but since this is a book for beginners, I'm going to share a few strategies you can get started with.

We're going to explore the following strategies with a little bit of detail throughout this chapter, but I highly recommend you note the strategies you like and then do your own research. See what they're all about and watch some videos to see if it's going to suit you.

Here are the strategies we're going to cover, followed by a detailed overview.

## The Breakout Strategy

A very popular trading strategy and a great way to make money in any duration of trading time, whether you're using this strategy multiple times per day, once a day, weekly, monthly, and so on. What you're basically doing is choosing a stock that is still in its early stages and is about to break out.

You can see when this is going to happen based on the chart data of a stock, which is why it's so important to practice your ability to read them. A 'breakout' occurs when a stock price is above a resistance level, or moves beneath a support line but still has increasing volume.

Stocks move up and down in value all the time and will have points where the breakout is beginning and then a point where the breakout will end. It's up to you when you choose to decide when to enter the market (at the beginning of the breakout) and when to leave (when the breakout is over or closing). I want to cover several strategies in this chapter, so I won't dive into the complexities of reading the charts to find these points, but do some research, learn the basics of this strategy and decide whether or not it's for you.

## The Scalping Strategy

Another fantastic trading strategy comes in the form of the scalping strategy. It is another one of the most popular strategies you'll see both beginner and experienced traders making the most of. The concept is simple. All you need to do is sell your stocks almost as soon as possible as they're making a profit.

The way scalping works is by letting yourself focus on the quantity of the trades you're making, rather than the quality. I'm not saying these aren't quality trades, but I am saying that instead of making one trade where you earn a 15% profit, you're making 15 trades that make a 1% profit.

That's actually a pretty spot-on example since most scalping traders will aim to sell stocks back after making a 1% profit. These trades will literally be made in a matter of minutes, so it's a very fast-paced strategy and a lot of fun to do.

A great way to ensure you can stick to this strategy is to set up tight stop orders through your brokerage software. This way, if a stock starts to fall instead of rising, you sell the stock back, thus minimizing your losses once again. Over time, with lots of little wins, you'll have the potential to make a sustainable profit.

## The Pivot Point Strategy

The Pivot Point Strategy has been used in the stock market for decades, so it's a tried and tested strategy that gets results when appropriately implemented. What is meant by the 'pivot point' is the median point of a stock value on its chart. With the median point in the middle of the chart, you'll have five support layers below and five levels of resistance above.

For a stock to be outside the pivot point range is incredibly rare since many traders will follow this strategy, which keeps the stock between these lines. The only real way you'll see an anomaly is on the freak day where the complete unexpected has occurred. It's sporadic to see.

As a trader, your job is to highlight these pivot points and make a purchase when the price is low, at the support line, and then sell them back when they're high, at the resistance line. This is a straightforward strategy, and you'll find that most brokerage software will actually have a feature that completes this strategy for you automatically, so it's well worth opening that up and giving it a try.

## The Momentum Strategy

Perhaps my personal favorite when it comes to stock market investment strategies, this is one of the most fun strategies, but maybe also the riskiest. Look at any stock market chart, and you'll see that it goes up and down all the time. As a momentum trader, all you're doing is riding the stock lines as it rises and then selling the stock back right at the peak before it falls.

Momentum is such a great day trading strategy because stocks can literally rise and fall throughout the day, meaning there are instant opportunities to make money. This may not seem like you're going to make a lot of money, but evidence shows that there is at least one stock every single day that will shift by around 20% to 30% in value.

So you see a stock you like, and you buy it at open for $1,000. The stock rises by 15% until around midday when it starts to drop. You sell the stocks, and you've just made $150, just like that. Of course, you could go to get lunch while your stocks are online and miss the drop and end up with a loss, which is just how volatile this strategy can be. However, if you're ready to be really engaged with your stocks and strategy, this is a great strategy to use, and it can be a really profitable one at that.

As I said at the beginning of this chapter, it's essential you take this information away and go and make up your own decision. Do your research and see what's out there, so you have the maximum chances to find the stock market strategy that's right for you.

# Day Seven — Defining Your Market Interest and Choosing your Stocks

In the last chapter, we took a look at a few of the strategies you're going to want to think about. While you may dedicate yourself to one strategy or could use multiple strategies, there's one key question you're going to be asking yourself. You've probably thought about this several times already.

Which stocks do you actually buy?

Choosing which stocks to buy is, of course, the aim of the game. It doesn't matter what strategy you're following since you're going to lose your investment if you pick the wrong stocks. There's a bit of an art or a knack to choosing stocks, and some key points you're going to want to think about, which is why I'm dedicating day seven to this process, detailing everything you need to know how to choose the right stocks to invest in.

## Take a Look, See What You Like

Perhaps the best way to choose stocks is to look into the stock market and see what there is. If you're reading this book, then I'm assuming you've at least spent some time looking at stocks and seeing what's out there, but I highly recommend taking a good few hours to get stuck in and see what's out there.

There's sure to be some golden stocks out there perfect for you that you don't even know exist yet. If you know about a specific company or are passionate about a particular industry, this can be a great place to start, but more on that shortly.

A really great way to find companies to invest in is to use an ETF, or exchange-traded fund. These are indexes that hold and track a list of companies who are trading on the stock market in a specific niche, and you can find out all about them.

For example, if you search 'tech ETF' online, you'll see a bunch of different ETFs come up, then you can just open them up and have a look through to see which stocks you like the look of.

## Look at the News and Follow the Trends

A great way to pick stocks is to see what's going on in the news and then making decisions based on this information. For example, if Apple is launching a brand-new iPhone, then the chances are, based on the history of the product, that it's going to be a success, thus raising the value of the stock. If you can invest in these stocks early, then you're going to make money off of them.

This is why it's so important to stay up to date with the news and media. Follow companies on social media within your chosen markets and see what they're up to. All of this information can come together to help you pick stocks that are best to buy.

We're going to talk a little more about this in the next chapter, but I just want to say that there are a plethora of ways you can go about this. You might tune into corporate presentations or live events to see what businesses are up to, as well as individual and commercial investor presentations, which will tell you which stocks the best of the best are interested in, a strategy which you can then emulate.

## Keep Your Portfolio Diverse

When you're starting out, you may not have any stocks in your portfolio, which is fine, but as you start adding and buying them in, you need to make sure you have diversity. Yes, it's important to knuckle down on a certain industry and market so you can learn about it inside out, but you also need a bit of variety.

I spoke about this before, but if you put all your eggs into one basket, and something bad happens, and you start experiencing a loss, then you're going to lose across the board. On the other hand, if you diverse and have stocks in a variety of markets, let's say three or four max, then you can minimize your losses in one market while making sure you have chances to still profit in others.

Another great way to do this is to get yourself a bunch of safe stocks, which are typically considered low-risk stocks. These are stocks where you know there's a very high chance you'll make money, although the profit won't be tremendous. Alongside these stocks, you can then get yourself a couple of high-risk stocks, or stocks that are going to have a big pay-out if they pay off.

## Always Look for the Story

Any good investor in the modern world will always be aware of what the story is behind the stock they're buying. By story, I mean the narrative behind a stock which defines why you're buying it. You need to ask yourself for the story every time you buy a stock and then judge how good that story is.

For example, you hear a piece of news that Apple is going to release a new phone. You do some research, and history shows that Apple stock has always risen when they've announced a new phone. This is your story, and it's a great way to justify why you're buying into a certain stock.

This method will also stop you from buying stocks just because it looks good'.

## Choose Stocks You Are Interested In

The final point to consider is that you should always choose stocks in a market you're actually interested in. You're going to be doing a ton of research, reading, and figuring out information in various markets and industries throughout your career. Since you're going to be spending so much time in this market, you may as well enjoy it.

If you don't enjoy the market or you don't have any kind of interest in it, you're going to become bored so quickly, and you'll end up making mistakes because you won't be fully committed to what you're doing. You'll do things like skim reading reports and not really taking in the information, which will lead to you making mistakes.

If you have a passion for conservation projects and sustainably saving the world, then look to invest in stocks in the sustainable energy industry, green energy, and recycling companies. You need to make sure you're connecting to the stocks you're choosing, or else you'll just go off investing in them and won't be as passionate as you could be.

Likewise, if you're interested in tech and loving reading up on all the latest gadgets and gizmos, then looking into stocks like Apple and Google will be far more beneficial to you than looking in stocks for companies like Walmart and the sorts. It's

always best to play to your strengths!

# Day Eight — Research Your Stocks

While in the last chapter, I talked about choosing which stocks you want. It's a whole other art form to actually researching the stocks and figuring out what's actually going on within that stock in relation to the market. Ultimately, the information you get from this chapter will define whether or not you think a stock will go up or down, therefore whether you're going to make any money from it.

Heading on from the last chapter, I'm going to assume you've done a bit of research and listed out a handful of stocks you like the look of, so now it's time to actually decide whether these are stocks you want to buy. Of course, this is an ongoing process, and while your research might say you don't want to buy a stock today, that doesn't mean you won't want to buy it tomorrow.

In the next few sections, I'm going to show you how to research your stocks and find information about them that can provide you with a solid understanding as to whether you should buy a stock or not. Let's go.

## Get to Know the Industry

While you should already be picking stocks in an industry you're passionate about, you need to know where a company sits within the industry and what the general consensus is towards that company. How do people see this company, and is it a company they like?

Who is your company's competition? How are they looked at by their customers and the rest of the market? Of course, if you're investing in a start-up company, you may hesitate because you're not sure whether it's going to be a successful company or not, but this kind of research will detail the surrounding market, so you can try and figure out where that company sits.

## Look at Individual Companies

Once you're happy with the company's position, now it's time to look at the company itself. Read customer reviews and look on social media for what is going on within that company. What are they working on? What products are they releasing?

Public companies allow you to see their financial documentation via the NASDAQ, or The National Association of Securities Dealer's Automated Quotation System. This governs the US stock regulator, and you'll be able to see the companies' financial reports that trade within it.

Depending on where you're trading in the world, you can access different versions of this. If you have a specific company in mind, just conduct an online search to see exactly what kind of financial status their company is in. If the company is massively in debt or is losing money over the years, it is probably not a good company to invest in.

## Look at the Internal Workings

Another way you can use the media to track a decision of whether you buy into a stock is by looking at what the company is up to internally. Has their marketing department just hired a hotshot marketing expert from another company? If so, this could be a sign that the stock is going to rise.

## Comparing the P/E Ratio

The P/E Ratio, which stands for the 'price-to-earnings ratio,' is a great figure to use when comparing similar companies within the same industry. It's always a good idea to compare other companies so you can see where your interested company stands. The lower the P/E ratio compared to the other similar companies, the better.

In fact, if a P/E ratio is really low, this is a great sign for investors, such as yourself, because it means the stock has been undervalued, and if you buy it now, you're going to make money on the stock when it regains its value. A 1:1 ratio means the stock is worth $1 for every dollar the company makes.

Alternatively, if the P/E ratio is 1:120, this means that a stock is worth $1 for every $120 the company makes, which is a huge undervalue. Over the next day or so, this will even itself out, and you'll make around $119 per stock you sell back once the price has corrected itself.

However, when comparing stocks between companies, if you see an above-average stock compared with competitors, this can also be a good sign. It shows that a company is doing really well and is above average, so it could definitely be worth investing in since it is a clear growth sign.

## Monitor the PEG Ratio

Another great figure to consider is the PEG ratio, which is a specific ratio that looks at a company's growth. It stands for Price-to-Earnings Growth and is worked out by dividing the

P/E ratio by the expected 12-month growth rate of the company stock value. If the ratio is less than 1.0, this is a positive growth company. If the ratio is more than 1.0, it's perhaps best off avoided.

If you can bear all these research strategies in mind, then you should have a very clear idea of whether buying a particular stock is a good idea. As I said before, this is an ongoing process, and there's a certain knack to being able to research properly and concisely. However, with a bit of time, practice, and experience, you'll be natural in no time at all!

# Day Nine — Making Your First Stock Investment

Well, today is the day you make your first stock investment. You've researched all the different companies; you've read the financial reports, and you know the story behind the stock you want to buy. You're ready to add to your portfolio, which is what this chapter is all about.

By now, you should have already set up your online broker account, so you'll want to sign into this via the website or software, so you're on the dashboard of your account. From here, it should be relatively easy to find the stock you want to buy simply using the abbreviated code. For example, Microsoft stocks are known as MSFT, so just search this to find the stock.

Once found, you'll then want to decide how many stocks you're going to buy. You could buy a single stock, or fill your entire portfolio; it's entirely up to you, but remember the advice I've given you so far. Many investors will only invest between 2% and 10% of their daily spending budget on one stock. Of course, this all depends on your strategy.

As your first stock, I highly recommend purchasing a single stock, just to get a feel for the buying process. Once you've done this a couple of times, you'll be familiar with the process, how long it takes, and what options you need to go through, and then you can comfortably move onto more substantial purchases.

As a new investor, you may also want to consider the latest introduction of fractional shares, which is something many modern stockbrokers will offer. For example, if you're buying a stock in Alphabet, the Google parent company, you'd be paying over $1,500 for a single share, which could be way too much.

Instead, fractional shares allow you to buy a portion of a single stock, which means you can start quickly investing in more prominent companies that typically have four-figure values.

## Defining Your Order Type

There are lots of different order types you need to be aware of, and when you get to this stage of the process for the first time, this is where you may be a little cautious and unsure what everything means. However, when you get here, just refer to the table below for a clear idea of what kind of order you want to make.

| A Market Order | This is the most common form of purchasing a stock where you'll simply choose your stock, place an order, and it will be added to your portfolio instantly. |
| --- | --- |
| | This kind of order is a guarantee that the execution of the order will take place, but it doesn't guarantee the price, so you'll always need to check before you confirm your sale. |

| A Limit Order | A limit order is the way you'll buy and sell a stock or other security at a specific price, guaranteeing the price in a way a market order cannot. |
|---|---|
| | For example, if you want to buy a stock for $10, you can activate a limit order to buy a stock at $10 and no other price. As long as the stock is over this price, the order won't execute, thus never guaranteeing the order will happen. |
| A Stop Order (A Stop-Loss Order) | This type of order is all about selling your stocks once it has reached a specific price threshold, known as the stop price. |
| | For example, if you want to sell a stock for $10, but it's currently worth £$8, you can activate a stop order, so when the stock does (perhaps) reach $10, it will create a market order and will sell. |
| A Buy Stop Order | Hand in hand with the Stop Loss Order, if you want to buy a stock at $10, but it's currently valued at $12, for example, you can activate a buy stop that will only create and execute a market order once a buy stop value has been reached. |

Don't get too worried about mastering all the basics and all the buying methods. There are a ton of complicated approaches you can take, but you really don't need to know them at this point. For many investors, they'll never move past market orders and limit orders, so there's no reason you need to.

So, once you've done this, all you need to do now is confirm your order, and the stock will be added to your portfolio! The money will come out of your account, and that's all you need to do! Congratulations, you've just purchased your first stock!

# Day Ten — Checking Your Facts

By now, you should be in a position where you're buying stocks for the first time, building up a little portfolio for yourself, and just getting to grips with how everything works and what it's like to be a stock trader. This may take a little while to get used to doing, like understanding what all the features are and how you're buying them, but this will all come naturally in time as you start developing your skills.

The next step is to really start knuckling down your process for choosing stocks in the first place. Of course, a few chapters back, I was talking to you about all the sources of information you can use to choose your stocks, but now I want to take things one step further.

Now we're going to be exploring the authenticity of your data and how to use fundamental analysis.

## What is Fundamental Analysis?

Let's start with the basics.

Fundamental analysis is simply the process of taking information from lots of various sources and evaluating this data to come to an answer for one simple question; is this stock going to make you any money?

For a complete overview, you're going to be looking at both qualitative data and quantitative data, and then using your own savvy and mindset to decide whether it's the right purchasing decision or not. Let's break it down a little further.

## What is Qualitative Data?

Qualitative Data is a type of data you're going to want to use when making your stock purchasing decisions. It basically refers to internal company 'things,' such as personnel positions within their company, any company news they release online or via press releases, and any financial events they are currently going through.

This kind of data also includes things like news reports offered out by journalists who share their opinions, the advice and recommendations from other traders, and large global events, like the COVID-19 pandemic or Brexit that could affect the value of a stock.

## What is Quantitative Data?

On the other hand, quantitative data could be referred to as the 'hard' data of a company. Some of the info you'll find under this kind of data includes;

- The earnings sheets of a company

- The balance sheets

- The ratios of a company

- The dividends it has to offer

Just to give you a complete and comprehensive into all the kinds of data, you refer back to the cheat sheet table I've created below.

| Company News | Qualitative | This is any news the company has released, such as information in a press release, on their website or blog, on their social media pages, or via a news article that the company has written. |
|---|---|---|
| Media News | Qualitative | Any news that has been written and released by a media company, such as a newspaper, business blog, or reporter. |
| Personnel Events | Qualitative | Events that happen within the company regarding their personnel structure and how they change. |
| Global Events | Quantitative | Events that happen around the world can affect any business, such as Brexit, COVID-19, or a presidential election. |

| Earnings Sheets | Quantitative | The sheets that detail a company's earnings, as part of fundamental analysis. |
|---|---|---|
| Balance Sheets | Quantitative | This list of figures details all the assets and liabilities a company has and the balance of all these different factors. |
| Dividends | Quantitative | This is the portion of money that a company will give back and pay-out to its shareholders without selling their shares back to them. |

## A Comprehensive Look into Ratios

I've spoken a little bit about ratios already, but they are one of the most important figures you're going to be looking at, which is why you need to understand what they are and how they affect a stock's value. Here's an insight into the most common ratios you'll use during your fundamental analysis process.

| | |
|---|---|
| **Price-to-Earnings Ratio (P/E)** | A simple metric that shows a stock's value relative to how the company makes a $1 in profit. This is an excellent ratio to use when comparing different companies within the same industry to see how they're performing. |
| **Debt-Equity Ratio (D/E)** | This ratio details how much debt a company has in relation to its assets, allowing you to easily compare these figures with similar companies within the same industry. |
| **Return on Equity (ROE)** | As the name suggests, this ratio compares the company and how profitable it can be against the equity it already owns. This figure is usually shown as a percentage. |
| **Current Ratio** | This ratio shows how capable a company is at being able to pay off and clear its debts, including the assets the company owns. |
| **Earnings Yield** | A figure that divides the earnings per share, known as the EPS, by the share price. If this figure is high, it means the stocks are undervalued. |
| **Price-earnings to Growth Ratio (PEG)** | This figure is calculated by taking the P/E ratio and comparing it against the percentage growth in the EPS. This is a great figure to use when choosing stocks because it shows the fair value of the stock. |

| | |
|---|---|
| **Relative Dividend Yield** | This ratio takes the company dividend yield and compares it to the entire rest of the index. This shows whether a company's stocks are overvalued or undervalued compared with competitors. |
| **Price-to-Book Ratio (P/B)** | A simple figure that compares the current market price of a stock against the book value of the company. A ratio larger than the sum of 1 means the shares are probably overvalued. |

## What's the Difference Between Fundamental and Technical Analysis?

In case you're wondering what the difference is between the two, I've written this section so we can get onto the same page. Both fundamental and technical analysis types of data that are used to help you know whether or not you want to choose and invest in a stock.

There's no right way or wrong way to use either analysis, nor is there one type of data that's better than the other, and there are some apparent differences between the two, which is what we're going to explore right now.

Technical analysis is the term given to the information that's on the stock market side of a company. You may look at performance indicators and price charts to see how a stock is performing in the market, especially when compared with competitors. You may also use oscillators to make your decisions.

On the other hand, fundamental analysis looks into the actual data the company has internally on itself. These could be raw company analysis data reports, or industry analysis. You may look at the forecasted profit of a company, and this would be using fundamental analysis.

As a short-term trader, like a day trader, you're going to edge towards using short-term technical analysis since you're comparing stocks against one another and against the market. If you're going for long-term investments, then you'll want the fundamental analysis to look into companies and their specifics.

## Is Your Information Accurate?

With all the information we've spoken about already, you need to ask yourself, for every single piece of information you're using to make your decision, is this information accurate?

For example, if you're searching online for data and come across the blog of another investor who says stock A will skyrocket in two days, what do you do? Do you run out and buy as much of that stock as possible? No, of course not. While it sounds exciting, how can you trust this information?

Go through the content and look for links and sources. Does the content link back to the company website or a bit of legitimate proof that the facts are real? If not, then get this information out of your head. It's not to be trusted, and it could end up with you making a wrong decision that's going to cost you real money you don't want to lose.

On the other hand, you're looking at the earnings sheets of a company that the company itself has released, and it's posted on all the official websites it should be posted on. Of course, this information is correct, so you can safely use it to make your decisions.

There are other ways you can check the legitimacy of your data. Unfortunately, it's essential you do take the time to check because there are blogs and websites out there that simply don't care whether you make money. They just want you to click on their website so they can sell ad space, so they will lie and create hype to get you onto their websites.

Just go through the content and see if it has any links to sources. If it doesn't, then it's probably made up. If you click on the author of a post (and if there's no exact author, then it's perhaps also a fake), see what posts they have written. If it's all clickbait and hysteria, then it's probably best off avoiding this writer altogether.

If you can do all this, and just use common sense while keeping your wits about you, then the chances are you'll only be using valid and correct data to base your decisions on. Always be mindful of where you're getting your data from. If you're spending thousands of dollars based on tips you heard from a city taxi driver, and you're not checking your sources, you're not going to last long in the stock market world.

# Day Eleven (Part One) — How to Read the Stock Markets

At this point, you've probably spent many an hour looking at charts, reading lists of stocks, and just generally finding your way around the technical side of the stock market. You've used a couple of brokers and decided which one you're going to stick with for now, and you've even got yourself some charting software.

While getting all these assets to help you make money is fantastic, it's a whole different ball game when it comes to actually reading the charts and the stock market itself. Many beginners will know a few bits here and there, but you'll soon be asking yourself, how do I actually read stocks?

# How Do I Read Stocks?

Stocks tend to come with two sources of information; a stock quote page and a stock chart. For live, real-time tracking of a stock value, you're going to want to look at the stock chart. It's here you'll see everything, including the price changes of the stock, the historical highs and lows of the stock (thus what the stock is capable of achieving), the trading volume, the dividends, the current trading price, and much more.

Don't let all this information put you off. It might seem a little overwhelming to begin with, but here's a table to describe the majority of the data you'll be working with.

| | |
|---|---|
| **52 Week High and Low** | This figure will show you the limits of a stock value over the course of the year. You'll see the highest value and the lowest value it has been. |
| **The Day High and Low** | The highest and lowest values of a stock over a trading day since opening, not 24 hours. |

| The Ticker Symbol | The ticker is the name for the code that describes the stock company. For example, Microsoft is MSFT, and Apple is AAPL. The New York Stock Exchange is NYSE. |
|---|---|
| P/E Ratio | The price-to-earnings ratio. You should know what this is by now! |
| The Dividend Yield | This the percentage return on a dividend, which is calculated by dividing the annual dividend by the real-time stock price. |
| Dividend Per Share | Dividends are the pay-outs that companies give to their shareholders. The higher the dividend, the healthier the company is because an unhealthy or struggling company will limit its dividend pay-outs. |
| The Open Price | The price in which the stock started at the open of the day. |
| The Close Price | The price value of the stock at the end of the day. |
| The Prev. Close Price | The price of the stock at the close the day before. |
| The Net Change Value | Whether a stock has increased or decreases in value, this figure will show the change difference at the end of close compared to the same value the day before. |

For now, I'm going to leave you with this, just because the layout of where you can find this information will differ depending on the broker software you're using, so it may take some time just to get your head around it all.

Don't forget to look into your strategy and see which of these figures and values you need to work out when you're going to buy and sell your stocks. The more familiar you can get with it all, the better off you'll be when it comes to working the markets and making money through your choices.

# Day Eleven (Part Two) — How to Read Stock Market Charts

When part one is familiar to you, it's time to work on your skills and abilities when it comes to reading charts. I remember when I looked at a stock market chart for the first time, and I had absolutely no idea what was going on. Anyway, let's get into learning how to read the charts.

## Looking at Prices and Time

On the right-hand side of the chart, you'll see the price, and the bar along the bottom is the time. This is pretty self-explanatory. Run your finger along the button to find the date and time you want and go up to see how much the stock cost at that time.

If you take a look at the bar on the top left, you'll notice you can change the date range of the bar to whatever you want, be it one day, three months, five years, ten years, or the maximum amount of data available.

If you're following this book and day trading, you'll want to set this date to the day or the month, so you quickly find the trends and patterns that are most recent.

## Look for Graph Trends

The black line you can see going through the middle of the graph is known as the trend line, and, as you can probably guess, the black line shows any trends that may be happening. For example, once a month before dividends are paid out, you may see a little spike in the value of the stock. If this happens every month for a year, you can guess this is probably a reliable trend.

You can change this line to look however you want, and it can tell you different stats. In the example above, this is a standard traditional line, but there are bar charts, line graphs, candlestick charts, and more. Here's a table explaining the differences;

| | |
|---|---|
| **Traditional Line** | Simply tracks the movements in the value of a stock over a length of time compared with the previous value on the last increment of time. |
| **Bar Chart** | A graph that shows the highest and lowest prices of a stock through a day, usually including the closing price of the stock as a trend. |
| **Candlestick Chart** | A little more complicated than the other kinds of chart, but usually uses green boxes to show when a stock closed higher than the previous day and a red box to show when it closed lower. Easy to see whether a stock is growing or decreasing in value over time. |

## Refer to the Trading Volume

At the bottom of the chart, you'll see another bar chart, and this refers to the volume of trades and stocks that are shifting for this stock. This is usually shown in both red and green bars. If the trading volume is high, or spikes, this will be shown in red and will mean that there's a lot of activity surrounding this stock.

For example, if the stock value drops but the volume is high, it means that there may be a definite downward trend, rather than the stock activity just having a little blip.

## Find the Resistance and Support Lines

Within every stock graph, you'll find a support line and a resistance line. Some lines you'll need to find yourself, whereas others will be displayed automatically on your charting software.

The resistance line refers to the very cap which the stock finds it hard to push through that value. On the other hand, the support line is like the bumper in which the value of the stock doesn't fall past. Of course, this figure can change all the time, but finding the line can be a great way to see what a stock is capable of doing, and what kind of value range you'll be working within.

# Day Twelve — Reinvesting Your Profits

We've spoken already in a previous chapter about how necessary it is to compound your investment profits, or in layman terms, make money on the money you make. As you trade stocks and start building up your portfolio, you're going to make money, but you can't just withdraw this money, put it straight into your bank account and then spend all it.

Well, you can, but this isn't a very good practice because you're going to limit your earnings drastically. Instead, you need to reinvest the money you make so that you can make even more money in much larger quantities. This is what it means to compound your earnings, and it's the strategy that has made Warren Buffett the powerhouse investor he is known for today.

But how do you do it? In this chapter, you'll find out.

First, let's look into a very basic example so that we're on the same page. Let's say you invest $10,000 into stocks. If you earn 5% profit on those earnings, in 20 years you'll be sitting on $26,533. If you double that to 10%, you'll have $67,275. With me so far?

If you really want to see what kind of earnings you can make, it's well worth searching online for a compound interest calculator where you can put in your own figures and have a play around with different numbers. This is a great thing to do when it comes to setting your portfolio goals and understanding what you're aiming for.

So, let's say you make $500 in your first month. Many people now will try and copy what they think top investors like Warren Buffett do and will invest this $500 is a handful of stocks that they believe will consistently do well. Think of large stocks like Apple and Microsoft. However, these are all stocks that have delivered in hindsight.

It's easy to pick stocks like Apple and Microsoft because they're already well known. What is much more difficult to do is to pick a stock in the same position as Apple or Microsoft was 20 years ago. If you can find stocks like this, then in 20 years' time, you'll have made a massive amount of profit by simply compounding your earnings.

Of course, there is the risk that you invest, and the stocks don't pay off, which ultimately compounds your earnings in the other direction. If you hold onto a stock for a long time and it doesn't pay off, this can be just as costly as not investing at all.

A great way to think about this to avoid losing money by picking the wrong stocks is to change your way of thinking. See your portfolio as a single asset, but instead, think of it as a living organism with many moving parts that are constantly changing and evolving. With this kind of mindset, you can make decisions that aim to keep your portfolio at its highest and healthiest possible condition.

We've spoken about this already, but it's such an important approach to remember. Rather than trying to continuously find new stocks to buy and add to your portfolio, instead focus on the stocks already within your portfolio that are doing well and then maximizing the profits you can get out of them. Likewise, highlight the stocks within your portfolio that are volatile or not doing so well, and clear them out, thus reducing your losses.

However, at some point, you are going to want to think about investing in new stocks because winning stocks don't last forever. We've already spoken in previous chapters about how you can find these, but there tend to be two main approaches you're going to want to consider.

The first, you can compound your earnings into long-term stocks. These are stocks that you think are going to pay off over the next 20 years or so and are going to bring in the big bucks. The other approach is simply to keep your profits in your day trading account and then simply reinvest them in the way that you've already been investing.

The biggest setback that most investors suffer from when it comes to compounding their profits and earnings is suffering too many problems and losses and not doing anything about it. When you're continually gambling on new stocks, firstly, you're not taking the time to really get to know the stocks you already have inside and out, but secondly, you're always opening yourself and your portfolio up to more risk and therefore more potential losses.

When you think about it, this makes sense. If you have five average stocks that are consistently doing well and have proven to do well over time, why would you then try and find new stocks to invest in, thus starting your risk factor high because you lack data on them? The majority of investors will let their greed get in the way here and will be looking for stocks that will give them a higher return in less time.

Remember, the key to success in the stock market world is acquiring lots of little wins over a long period of time. You'll rarely see someone make one big win overnight. It doesn't happen, but you need to be investing a ton of money in the first place for that to happen.

## Don't Forget to Live

Of course, it's important to remember that you do need to live, and if you're investing on the stock market as your full-time career, then you need to pay yourself a wage. It can be tempting to reinvest all your earnings back into your portfolio but try to find balance.

Set yourself a budget and see how much of your account balance you want to withdraw and how much you want to reinvest. There's no right or wrong way of doing this, so figure out what works for you. If you're investing as a side hustle and continuing your full-time job, then you could even compound the lot!

So, to summarise this chapter, reinvesting your profits and earnings is a great idea, and it's how you're going to grow your portfolio to become bigger and bigger over time. However, you don't want to continuously look for new stocks to invest in over and over again, but instead, double down on the successful stocks you already know about.

When it does come a time to look for new stocks, either continue the practices you're already using to make money, i.e., day trading with large daily limits and allowances, or look into long-term stocks that can make money over several decades, effectively expanding and diversifying your portfolio.

# Day Thirteen — Looking to the Future and Expanding Your Horizons

And so, you've nearly come to the end of your journey, but while we've been exploring all the basics and fundamentals that you need to know when it comes to going from a complete beginner to the stock market to somewhat of a master, it wouldn't be right to leave without thinking about your future.

Depending on your personal situation at present, it's very possible you can go from zero to hero in just 14 days, perhaps sooner, but perhaps longer. It's important that you don't rush your journey into the trading world, but instead take your time, look at it all from different angles, and master the skills you need to know.

But, while focusing on what you can do better now, it's important to take some time to see how you're going to improve in the future. What tips are there to help you grow as a trader and to better your skills, and ultimately to grow your portfolio in the healthiest possible way. This is what I'm going to be focusing on this in this chapter, so let's not mess around.

## Get Educated

We live in modern times, and there are many resources out there to help you learn tactics and strategies to improve your ability to handle emotional situations and better your decision-making process. Whatever you want to know, a quick online search will give you more content than you can ever read.

Whether you're reading blogs from other investors, looking at trading websites, using online mentors, watching YouTube videos, or even getting involved in coaching courses, you need to invest time in learning if you want to get better.

I'm not saying that real-world experience isn't important. It's crucial.

You can't just spend hours and hours reading and watching content to help you become a better trader and then expect you're going to know everything. Real-world experience and getting educated go hand in hand, and you can't have one without the other.

It's like any skill in life, you just need to repeat the same thing over and over again, and you'll start to get better. If you're a bit cautious with your approach, that's fine and perfectly understandable. If this sounds like you, then I highly recommend opening a demo trading account that uses fake money.

This way, you can practice certain components of trading and see how you'll do. You can test different strategies using real-world data to see how they work and whether it's a strategy you want to use. This way, you can take risks and see the outcome without actually losing or winning any money. It's a great way to master the basics and to get you familiar with what you're doing.

When you couple this with the education you'll receive from places like this book and the internet, which will help guide you in the right direction, you'll be progressing at a very positive pace. Don't forget, if you have any questions or make a mistake and unsure what went wrong, then always take time to look it up and learn. Never just brush it off and hope it doesn't happen again.

While on the subject of practicing, most investors will also recommend that you spend around six months planning and utilizing your strategy. You work on a particular part of your plan, and then you implement it, master it, and then move onto the next. Six months is a decent time period because you'll see explosive days, quiet ranges, volatile days, and everything in between.

This means when you get to the end of the six months, you'll already know that your trading plan has what it takes to get you through anything.

Knowledge truly is power!

## Self-Evaluate Your Practices

Hand in hand with the consideration above, it's a common process for traders to finish a day of trading and then look back on what they did and the decisions they've made to evaluate how they performed, what they did good, and what they can do better. Notice how I'm not saying to 'critic' yourself.

Say you lose some money and you get emotional about it. It happens to the best of us. This leads to you making some bad decisions throughout the rest of the day, and you end the day in a bad place. It's a good idea to build the habit of reviewing your decisions and processes at the end of each and every day. Never missing a day means you're always going to be improving. You may want to keep a journal for this, especially since it's easy to look back on.

As above, you need to practice evaluating yourself at the end of every single day and make sure you're honest about what you write. If you're not, well, you're only going to be harming yourself and your own improvement journey. You also need to ensure you're reviewing your trading plan and strategy, but this can be done on a weekly or monthly basis.

Really go into detail when reviewing yourself. Look at every trade and figure out the story behind it. Ask yourself why you made that decision and what fuelled it. If it was a bad decision, figure out where you went wrong. Likewise, if it was a good decision, evaluate what you did right so you can keep doing that.

## Actually Updating Your Trading Plan

Let's say you're copying the trading strategy of a well-known investor, and it's not quite working out. You look at your plan and review it, and you notice a series of decisions where you messed up and some days that were just unlucky, but you let it slide and keep on sticking with the plan.

Why are you doing this? Just because the top investor told you so?

Sure, it's great to emulate plans and strategies, but it's important for your learning and your progress that you edit these strategies to suit you and your personal financial requirements and goals. If you see some problems with your plan, even if it's an emulated plan, don't be afraid to make changes to make things better.

Far too many people have a plan and stick to it religiously, and this is where the 'oh, the market must be rigged, and against me' attitude comes in. What these people don't realize is that their plans and strategies need to move with the times, just like the markets do.

The world, in particular the financial world, is changing all the time, and the way traders interact with the market needs to change alongside this. I highly recommend only focusing on one issue at a time that pops up with your daily reviews, rather than trying to change a whole bunch of things.

This approach just gets confusing and messy, and you don't actually know what specific thing you have then changed that makes things better or worse. Changing one thing at a time allows you to focus on the details of your trading strategy by making small adjustments and tweaks that perfect your strategy again and again.

While I would recommend focusing on the basics for now, it's always a great idea to build a habit of reviewing yourself and evaluating your processes early on because it's something you're going to need to do solidly in the future. I'm not saying you need to be hard on yourself, nor should you be a perfectionist. You just evaluate and aim to get 1% better every day.

# Day Fourteen — Final Thoughts and Summary

And with that, we come to the end of your journey, and now it's all over to you! How exciting has this journey been, and how much have you learned? As I said in the introduction, the whole aim of this book was to introduce all the concepts you need to know when it comes to going from being a beginner trader to a professional.

Just keep refining your skills, learning and mastering your processes, educating yourself, and evaluating, and you'll see yourself take great and beautiful strides in the world of investing, thus making passive income and sustainably growing your portfolio. What a beautiful world we live in where this can be an opportunity for you to work for yourself.

If you have found some good uses for this book, I'd love to hear from you. Please leave me some reviews online, so I know what you think and can continue to write these books down in the future. I've poured my heart and soul into these books to try and share my own experiences of the world so you can enjoy your own in the best possible way, and it's incredibly motivating to hear that they're doing their job!

In the meantime, keep up to date with the markets, and I wish you the best of luck on your journey. The world of being a stock trader is not an easy world to crack, and like everything in life, it requires a certain investment of time and money. Dedicate yourself fully, and the rewards will be bright and beautiful!

Best of luck!

Printed in Great Britain
by Amazon